SEVEN STEPS TO MONETIZE FREE EARNED NFT.

Edit with WPS Office

Copyright © 2010 by Michael Quirk

All rights reserved. No part of this publication may be reproduced, distributed, or transmitted in any form or by any means, including photocopying, recording, or other electronic or mechanical methods, without the prior written permission of the publisher, except in the case of brief quotations embodied in critical reviews and certain other noncommercial uses permitted by copyright law.

Edit with WPS Office

Table of content

Edit with WPS Office

INTRODUCTION

Envision purchasing a piece of computerized craftsmanship on the Internet at a sensible cost and getting an interesting advanced token realized which demonstrates your position over the fine art you purchased. Couldn't it be perfect? Indeed, that open door exists currently, on account of NFTs.

NFTs are as of now taking the advanced craftsmanship and collectables world by storm. Similarly as everybody overall accepted Bitcoin was the advanced solution to money, NFTs are presently pitched as the computerized reply to collectibles. Asa result, computerized specialists are seeing their lives changing thanks to the huge deals to a new crypto crowd.

To investigate more about what they are, you have come to the ideal locations. We should make a plunge and see what's going on with all the quarrel!

Edit with WPS Office

CHAPTER ONE

What is NFT?

NFT implies non-fungible tokens (NFTs), which are by and large made utilizing a similar kind of programming utilized for digital currencies. In straightforward terms these cryptographic resources depend on blockchain innovation. They can't be traded or exchanged comparably like other cryptographic resources.

Like Bitcoin or Ethereum. The term NFT obviously addresses it can nor be supplanted nor exchanged in light of the fact that it has one of a kind properties. Actual cash and digital currency are fungible, and that implies that they can be exchanged or traded for each other.

NFT represents a non-fungible token, and that implies it can nor be supplanted nor exchanged on the grounds that it has interesting properties.

Key Features of NFT -

Computerized Asset - NFT is a computerized resource that addresses Internet collectibles like craftsmanship, music, and games with a bona fide testament made by blockchain innovation that underlies Cryptocurrency.

Edit with WPS Office

One of a kind - It can't be fashioned or generally controlled.

Trade - NFT trades happen with digital forms of money, for example, Bitcoin on expert locales.

Cryptopunks is a striking illustration of a NFT. It empowers you to purchase, sell and store 10,000 collectibles with confirmation of-possession.

A NFT (Non-fungible token) is a record on a blockchain which is related with a specific computerized or actual resource. The responsibility for NFT is kept in the blockchain, and can be moved by the proprietor, permitting NFTs to be sold and exchanged. NFTs can be made by anyone, and require not many or no coding abilities to make. NFTs regularly contain references to computerized documents, for example, photographs, recordings, and sound. Since NFTs are interestingly recognizable resources, they vary from digital forms of money, which are fungible.

Representation of a non-fungible token produced by a brilliant agreement (a program intended to consequently execute contract terms)

Defenders of NFTs guarantee that NFTs give a public endorsement of validness or evidence of possession, however the legitimate freedoms conveyed by a NFT can be unsure. The responsibility for NFT as characterized by the blockchain has no intrinsic lawful significance, and doesn't be guaranteed to allow

Edit with WPS Office

copyright, licensed innovation freedoms, or other legitimate privileges over its related advanced record. A NFT doesn't limit the sharing or duplicating of its related computerized record, and doesn't forestall the making of NFTs that reference indistinguishable documents.

The NFT market developed decisively from 2020-2021: the exchanging of NFTs in 2021 expanded to more than $17 billion, up by 21,000% more than 2020's all out of $82 million. NFTs have been utilized as speculative ventures, and they have drawn expanding analysis for the energy cost and carbon impression related with approving blockchain exchanges as well as their successive use in craftsmanship tricks. The NFT market has likewise been contrasted with a monetary air pocket or a Ponzi conspire. By May 2022, the NFT market was viewed as falling.

How Does NFT Work?

Now that you've made your underlying strides in understanding what a NFT is, you ought to forge ahead and find out about how a NFT functions.

Most of NFTs dwell on the Ethereum digital currency's blockchain, a circulated public record that records exchanges.

NFTs are individual tokens with significant data put away in them.

Since they hold a worth fundamentally set by the market and request, they can be traded very much like other actual kinds of craftsmanship.

Edit with WPS Office

NFTs' novel information makes it simple to check and approve their possession and the exchange of tokens between proprietors.

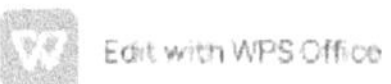
Edit with WPS Office

CHAPTER TWO

NFTs (non-fungible tokens) are extraordinary cryptographic tokens that exist on a blockchain and can't be duplicated.

NFTs can address genuine things like work of art and land.

"Tokenizing" these certifiable unmistakable resources makes purchasing, selling, and exchanging them more productive while lessening the likelihood of misrepresentation.

NFTs can likewise work to address people's characters, property privileges, and that's just the beginning.

A NFT is a unit of information, put away on a sort of computerized record called a blockchain, which can be sold and exchanged. The NFT can be related with a specific computerized or actual resource like pictures, craftsmanship, music, and game features and may give permitting freedoms to involve the resource for a predetermined reason. A NFT (and, if material, the related permit to utilize, duplicate, or show the hidden resource) can be exchanged and sold on advanced markets. The unprecedented idea of NFT exchanging as a rule brings about a casual trade of responsibility for resource that has no legitimate reason for implementation, thus frequently presents minimal more than use as a superficial point of interest.

NFTs capability like cryptographic tokens, yet dissimilar to digital forms of money, for example, Bitcoin or Ethereum, NFTs are not tradable together, as are not fungible. (While all bitcoins are

Edit with WPS Office

equivalent, each NFT might address an alternate basic resource and in this manner might have an alternate worth.) NFTs are made when blockchains connect records containing cryptographic hashes — sets of characters that distinguish a bunch of information — onto past records, making a chain of recognizable information blocks. This cryptographic exchange process guarantees the confirmation of each computerized file[clarification needed] by giving an advanced mark that tracks NFT proprietorship. Information connects that are important for NFT records, that for instance might highlight insights regarding where the related workmanship is put away, can be impacted by interface decay.

NFT is ownable, the resource connection might be ownable, and the resources proprietorship isn't ensured

A chart showing the option to claim of a non-fungible token and connected record. Generally speaking, it is vigorously reliant upon the symbolic's shrewd agreement.

A NFT exclusively addresses a proof of responsibility for blockchain record, and doesn't be guaranteed to infer that the proprietor has licensed innovation privileges to the computerized resource the NFT indicates to address. Somebody might sell a NFT that addresses their work, however the purchaser won't be guaranteed to get copyright to that work, and the dealer may not be disallowed from making extra NFT duplicates of a similar work. As per lawful researcher Rebecca Tushnet, "In one sense, the buyer obtains anything that the craftsmanship world thinks they

Edit with WPS Office

have gained. They most certainly don't claim the copyright to the fundamental work except if it is expressly moved."

Certain NFT projects, like Bored Apes, unequivocally relegate protected innovation privileges of individual pictures to their particular proprietors. The NFT assortment CryptoPunks was an undertaking that at first disallowed proprietors of its NFTs from involving the related computerized fine art for business use, however later permitted such use upon a securing of the assortment's parent organization.

NFTs have the potential for a few use cases. For instance, they are an optimal vehicle to carefully address actual resources like land and craftsmanship. Since they depend on blockchains, NFTs can likewise attempt to eliminate mediators and interface craftsmen with crowds or for character the executives. NFTs can eliminate mediators, improve on exchanges, and make new business sectors.

A significant part of the ongoing business sector for NFTs is based on collectibles, for example, computerized work of art, sports cards, and rarities. Maybe the most advertised space is NBA Top Shot, a spot to gather non-fungible tokenized NBA minutes in computerized card structure. A portion of these cards have sold for a great many dollars.

Edit with WPS Office

As of late, Twitter's (TWTR) Jack Dorsey tweeted a connection to a tokenized variant of the very first tweet, in which he expressed: "simply setting up my twttr." The NFT rendition of the very first tweet sold for more than $2.9 million.

$69 million

Toward the beginning of March 2021, a gathering of NFTs by computerized craftsman Beeple sold for more than $69 million. The deal set a trend and a record for the most costly bits of computerized craftsmanship sold up to this point. The craftsmanship was a composition involved Beeple's initial 5,000 days of work.

Like actual cash, digital currencies are fungible, implying that they can be exchanged or traded, one for another. For instance, one bitcoin is generally equivalent in worth to another bitcoin. Essentially, a solitary unit of ether is dependably equivalent to another unit. This fungibility trademark makes cryptographic forms of money reasonable as a safe mechanism of exchange in the computerized economy.

NFTs shift the crypto worldview by making every symbolic remarkable and indispensable, consequently making it unimaginable for one non-fungible token to be equivalent to another. They are computerized portrayals of resources and have

Edit with WPS Office

been compared to advanced international IDs on the grounds that every token contains a novel, non-adaptable character to recognize it from different tokens. They are likewise extensible, meaning you can join one NFT with one more to "breed" a third, remarkable NFT.

Very much like Bitcoin, NFTs additionally contain possession subtleties for simple distinguishing proof and move between token holders. Proprietors can likewise add metadata or characteristics relating to the resource in NFTs. For instance, tokens addressing espresso beans can be delegated fair exchange. Or on the other hand, specialists can sign their advanced craftsmanship with their own particular in the metadata.

Edit with WPS Office

CHAPTER THREE

Types of NFT

The NFT world is somewhat new to individuals. Here are a few instances of NFTs that exist today:

A Digital Collectible

Area Names

Games

Expositions

Tennis shoes in design line

What is NFT Used For?

Individuals inspired by Crypto-exchanging and individuals who like to gather fine art frequently use NFTs. Other than that, it has a few different purposes excessively like:

Advanced Content - The main utilization of NFTs today is in computerized content. Content makers see their benefits upgraded by NFTs, as they power a maker economy where makers have the responsibility for content over to the stages they use to expose it.

Gaming Items - NFTs have gathered extensive interest from game

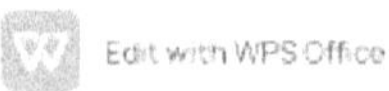
Edit with WPS Office

designers. NFTs can give a ton of advantages to the players. Regularly, in a web based game, you can purchase things for your personality, however that is the end of the line. With NFTs, you can recover your cash by selling the things whenever you're done with them.

Venture and Collaterals - Both NFT and DeFi (Decentralized Finance) share a similar foundation. DeFi applications let you get cash by utilizing insurance. NFT and DeFi both work together to investigate involving NFTs as insurance all things considered.

Space Names - NFTs furnish your area with a more straightforward to-recall name. This works like a site space name, making its IP address more significant and important, generally founded on length and pertinence.

Indeed, even big names like Snoop Dogg, Shawn Mendes, and Jack Dorsey are looking into the NFT by delivering exceptional recollections and fine art and selling them as securitized NFTs.

NBA Top Shot Is a Hot NFT Use Case

One of the most well known non-fungible tokens lately is NBA Top Shot, an organization between Dapper Labs (producers of the CryptoKitties game) and the National Basketball Association

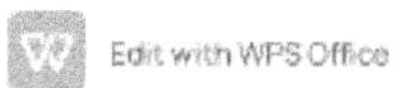
Edit with WPS Office

(NBA). The NBA licenses individual feature video reels, among other substance, to Dapper Labs, and they digitize the recording and make it ready to move to buyers. Each reel shows a video cut, for example, a well known player's ball dunk, some including various points and computerized craftsmanship to make them remarkable. Regardless of whether somebody made an ideal duplicate of the video, it tends to be in a split second conspicuous as a fake. The endeavor has previously produced $230 million in deals, and the organization just likewise gotten $305 million in subsidizing from a gathering that incorporates Michael Jordan and Kevin Durant.

These video reels are selling at exorbitant costs. Among the most famous:

LeBron James "Grandiose" Dunk: $208,000

Zion Williamson "Holo MMXX" Block: $100,000

LeBron James "From the Top" Block: $100,000

LeBron James "Throwdowns" Dunk: $100,000

LeBron James "Holo MMXX" Dunk: $99,999

Steph Curry "Deck the Hoops" Handles: $85,000

Giannis Antetokounmpo "Holo MMXX" Dunk: $85,000

LeBron James "From the Top" Dunk: $80,000

Edit with WPS Office

These special NBA minutes are printed and delivered into the commercial center through "pack drops." The most widely recognized sell for just nine bucks, however more restrictive packs can sell for significantly more.

Now that you've perceived what is NFT utilized for, and the different ways you can profit from it, we should investigate how it is explicitly unique in relation to different structures on digital money.

Regularly related documents

NFTs have been utilized to trade computerized tokens that connect to an advanced record resource. Responsibility for NFT is frequently connected with a permit to utilize such a connected computerized resource, yet for the most part doesn't give copyright to the purchaser. A few arrangements just award a permit for individual, non-business use, while different licenses likewise permit business utilization of the hidden computerized resource.

Advanced craftsmanship

Computerized craftsmanship is a typical use case for NFTs. High-profile closeouts of NFTs connected to computerized craftsmanship certainly stand out. The work entitled Merge by craftsman Pak was the most costly NFT, with a closeout cost of

Edit with WPS Office

US$91.8 million[41] and Everydays: the First 5000 Days, by craftsman Mike Winkelmann (referred to expertly as Beeple) the second generally costly at US$69.3 million out of 2021.

Some computerized craftsmanship NFTs, similar to these pixel workmanship characters, are instances of generative workmanship.

Some NFT assortments, including Bored Apes, EtherRocks and CryptoPunks are instances of generative workmanship, where a wide range of pictures are made by gathering a choice of basic picture parts in various mixes.

In March 2021, the blockchain organization Injective Protocol purchased a $95,000 unique screen print entitled Morons (White) from English spray painting craftsman Banksy, and shot someone copying it with a cigarette lighter. They minted[jargon] and sold the video as a NFT. The individual who obliterated the craftsmanship, who referred to themselves as "Consumed Banksy", portrayed the go about as a method for moving an actual masterpiece to the NFT space.

American custodian and craftsmanship student of history Tina Rivers Ryan, who represents considerable authority in advanced works, said that workmanship exhibition halls are broadly not persuaded that NFTs have "enduring social relevance."Ryan

Edit with WPS Office

analyzes NFTs to the net craftsmanship trend before the website bubble. No unified method for confirmation exists to keep taken and fake computerized works from being sold as NFTs, in spite of the fact that closeout houses as christie Sotheby's, and different exhibition halls and displays overall began joint efforts and organizations with advanced specialists, for example, Refik Anadol, Dangiuz and Sarah Zucker, selling NFTs related with advanced fine arts (by means of NFT stages) and displaying those craftsmanships (related with the particular NFTs) both in virtual displays and genuine screens, screens, and TVs.

Mars House, a structural NFT made in May 2020 by craftsman Krista Kim, sold in 2021 for 288 Ether (ETH) — around then comparable to US$524,558.

Games

Primary article: Blockchain game

NFTs can address in-game resources, like advanced plots of land. A few observers depict these as being controlled "by the client" rather than the game engineer on the off chance that they can be exchanged on outsider commercial centers without consent from the game designer.

CryptoKitties was an early fruitful blockchain web based game in which players embrace and exchange virtual felines. The

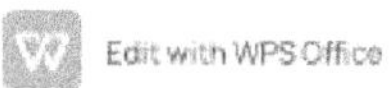
Edit with WPS Office

adaptation of NFTs inside the game raised a $12.5 million venture, for certain kitties selling for more than $100,000 each. Following its prosperity, CryptoKitties was added to the ERC-721 norm, which was made in January 2018 (and concluded in June). A comparative NFT-based web based game, Axie Infinity, was sent off in March 2018.

In October 2021, Valve Corporation restricted applications from their Steam stage assuming that those applications use blockchain innovation or NFTs to trade worth or game antiquities.

In December 2021, Ubisoft reported Ubisoft Quartz, "a NFT drive which permits individuals to purchase falsely scant advanced things utilizing digital currency". The declaration was vigorously censured by crowds, with the Quartz declaration video achieving an aversion proportion of 96% on YouTube. Ubisoft would later unlist the video from YouTube. The declaration was likewise censured inside by Ubisoft designers. The Game Developers Conference's 2022 yearly report expressed that 70% of engineers reviewed said their studios cared very little about incorporating NFTs or digital money into their games.

Some extravagance brands stamped NFTs for online computer game beauty care products. In November 2021, venture company Morgan Stanley distributed a note guaranteeing that this could turn into a US$56 billion dollar market by 2030.

In July 2022, Mojang Studios reported that NFTs wouldn't be allowed in Minecraft, saying that they conflicted with the game's "upsides of imaginative consideration and playing together".

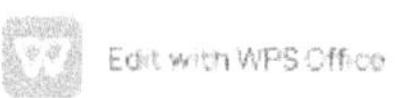
Edit with WPS Office

Music

In February 2021, NFTs purportedly produced around US$25 million in the music business, with specialists selling fine art and music as NFT tokens. On February 28, 2021, electronic dance performer 3LAU sold an assortment of 33 NFTs for a sum of US$11.7 million to recognize the three-year commemoration of his Ultraviolet collection. On March 3, 2021, a NFT was made to advance the Kings of Leon collection When You See Yourself. Different performers who have utilized NFTs incorporate American rapper Lil Pump, Grimes, visual craftsman Shepard Fairey in a joint effort with record maker Mike Dean, and rapper Eminem.

Film

In May 2018, twentieth Century Fox collaborated with Atom Tickets and delivered restricted release Deadpool 2 computerized banners to advance the film. They were accessible from OpenSea and the GFT trade. In March 2021 Adam Benzine's 2015 narrative Claude Lanzmann: Specters of the Shoah turned into the primary movie and narrative film to be unloaded as a NFT.

Different tasks in the entertainment world utilizing NFTs incorporate the declaration that a selective NFT fine art assortment will be delivered for Godzilla versus Kong and chief Kevin Smith reporting in April 2021 that his impending blood and gore flick Killroy Was Here would be delivered as a NFT. The 2021 movie Zero Contact, coordinated by Rick Dugdale and featuring

Edit with WPS Office

Anthony Hopkins, was likewise delivered as a NFT.

In April 2021, a NFT related with the score of the film Triumph, made by Gregg Leonard, was the principal NFT stamped for a component film score.

In November 2021, movie chief Quentin Tarantino delivered seven NFTs in view of whole scenes of Pulp Fiction. Miramax in this manner documented a claim guaranteeing that their film privileges were disregarded and that the first 1993 agreement with Tarantino gave them the option to mint NFTs corresponding to Pulp Fiction.

Other related records

Various web images have been related with NFTs, which were stamped and sold by their makers or by their subjects. Models incorporate Doge, a picture of a Shiba Inu canine, as well as Charlie Bit My Finger, Nyan Cat and Disaster Girl.

A few virtual universes, frequently showcased as metaverses, have integrated NFTs for the purpose of exchanging virtual things and virtual land.

A few obscene works have been sold as NFTs, however aggression from NFT commercial centers towards explicit material has introduced huge downsides for makers.

In May 2021, UC Berkeley reported that it would sell NFTs for the patent revelations for two Nobel Prize-winning creations: CRISPR-Cas9 quality altering and malignant growth immunotherapy. The college will keep on claiming the licenses for these developments;

Edit with WPS Office

the NFTs relate just to the college patent exposure structure, an inward structure involved by the college for scientists to reveal innovations.

The main credited political dissent NFT ("Destruction of Nazi Monument Symbolizing Contemporary Lithuania") was a video recorded by Professor Stanislovas Tomas on April 8, 2019, and printed on March 29, 2021. In the video, Tomas utilizes a demolition hammer to obliterate a state-supported Lithuanian plaque situated on the Lithuanian Academy of Sciences respecting Nazi conflict criminal Jonas Noreika.

In 2020, CryptoKitties engineer Dapper Labs delivered the NBA TopShot project, which permitted the acquisition of NFTs connected to b-ball highlights.[88] The venture was based on top of the Flow blockchain.

In March 2021 a NFT of Twitter pioneer Jack Dorsey's very first tweet sold for $2.9 million. A similar NFT was recorded available to be purchased in 2022 at $48 million, yet just accomplished a top bid of $280.

Edit with WPS Office

CHAPTER FOUR

The first known "NFT", Quantum, was made by Kevin McCoy and Anil Dash in May 2014. It comprises of a video cut made by McCoy's significant other, Jennifer. McCoy enrolled the video on the Namecoin blockchain and offered it to Dash for $4, during a live show for the Seven on Seven gathering at the New Museum in New York City. McCoy and Dash alluded to the innovation as "adapted illustrations". This expressly connected a non-fungible, tradable blockchain marker to a masterpiece, by means of on-chain metadata (empowered by Namecoin). This is as opposed to the multi-unit, fungible, metadata-less "hued coins" of other blockchains and Counterparty.

In October 2015, the primary NFT project, Etheria, was sent off and exhibited at DEVCON 1 in London, Ethereum's most memorable engineer meeting, 90 days after the send off of the Ethereum blockchain. A large portion of Etheria's 457 available and tradable hexagonal tiles went unsold for over five years until March 13, 2021, when recharged interest in NFTs ignited a purchasing furor. In the span of 24 hours, all tiles of the ongoing variant and an earlier rendition, each hardcoded to 1 ETH (US$0.43 at the hour of send off), were sold for a sum of US$1.4 million.

The expression "NFT" just accomplished more extensive use with the ERC-721 norm, first proposed in 2017 by means of the

Edit with WPS Office

Ethereum GitHub, following the send off of different NFT projects that year. The standard harmonized with the send off of a few NFT projects, including Curio Cards, CryptoPunks (a task to exchange remarkable animation characters, delivered by the American studio Larva Labs on the Ethereum blockchain), and intriguing Pepe exchanging cards.

The 2017 internet game CryptoKitties was made productive by selling tradable feline NFTs, and its prosperity carried public regard for NFTs.

The NFT market experienced fast development during 2020, with its worth significantly increasing to US$250 million. In the initial three months of 2021, a greater number of than US$200 million were spent on NFTs.

In 2020, the U.S Patent and Trademark Office got three brand name applications for NFTs. In 2021, the quantity of brand name applications leaped to more than 1200. In January 2022, the U.S. Patent and Trademark Office got 450 NFT-related brand name applications. The developing rundown of brands being reserved for NFTs incorporates the NYSE, Star Trek, Panera, Walmart, Elvis Presley, Sports Illustrated, Ticketmaster, and Yahoo. In the early long stretches of 2021, interest in NFTs expanded after various high-profile deals and workmanship barters.

Edit with WPS Office

In May 2022, The Wall Street Journal detailed that the NFT market was "imploding". Day to day deals of NFT tokens had declined 92% from September 2021, and the quantity of dynamic wallets in the NFT market fell 88% from November 2021. While increasing loan costs had influenced unsafe wagers across the monetary business sectors, the Journal said "NFTs are among the most speculative."

Explicit symbolic norms support different blockchain use-cases. Ethereum was the first blockchain to help NFTs with its ERC-721 norm and this is currently[may be obsolete as of March 2022] the most broadly utilized. Numerous other blockchains have added or plan to add support for NFTs.

ERC-721 was the main norm for addressing non-fungible computerized resources on the Ethereum blockchain. ERC-721 is an inheritable Solidity shrewd agreement standard; "inheritable" implies that designers can make new ERC-721-consistent agreements by replicating from a reference execution. ERC-721 gives center techniques that permit following the proprietor of an exceptional identifier, as well as a permissioned way for the proprietor to move the resource for other people.

The ERC-1155 standard offers "semi-fungibility", as well as giving a simple to ERC-721 usefulness (implying that an ERC-721 resource can be fabricated utilizing ERC-1155). Not at all like ERC-

Edit with WPS Office

721 where an exceptional ID addresses a solitary resource, the remarkable ID of an ERC-1155 token addresses a class of resources, and there is an extra amount field to address how much the class that a specific wallet has. Resources of a similar class are compatible, and a client can move any measure of resources for other people.

Other related documents

Various web images have been related with NFTs, which were printed and sold by their makers or by their subjects. Models incorporate Doge, a picture of a Shiba Inu canine, as well as Charlie Bit My Finger, Nyan Cat and Disaster Girl.

A few virtual universes, frequently promoted as metaverses, have consolidated NFTs for the purpose of exchanging virtual things and virtual land.

A few obscene works have been sold as NFTs, however antagonism from NFT commercial centers towards explicit material has introduced critical downsides for makers.

In May 2021, UC Berkeley declared that it would sell NFTs for the patent exposures for two Nobel Prize-winning creations: CRISPR-Cas9 quality altering and malignant growth immunotherapy. The college will keep on possessing the licenses for these creations; the NFTs relate just to the college patent revelation structure, an inside structure involved by the college for scientists to unveil developments.

The primary credited political dissent NFT ("Destruction of Nazi Monument Symbolizing Contemporary Lithuania") was a video

Edit with WPS Office

shot by Professor Stanislovas Tomas on April 8, 2019, and stamped on March 29, 2021. In the video, Tomas utilizes a demolition hammer to obliterate a state-supported Lithuanian plaque situated on the Lithuanian Academy of Sciences respecting Nazi conflict criminal Jonas Noreika.

In 2020, CryptoKitties designer Dapper Labs delivered the NBA TopShot project, which permitted the acquisition of NFTs connected to b-ball features. The task was based on top of the Flow blockchain.

In March 2021 a NFT of Twitter organizer Jack Dorsey's very first tweet sold for $2.9 million. A similar NFT was recorded available to be purchased in 2022 at $48 million, yet just accomplished a top bid of $280.

Hypothesis

NFTs addressing computerized collectables and craftsmanships are a speculative resource. The NFT purchasing flood was called a financial air pocket by specialists, who additionally contrasted it with the Dot-com bubble. In March 2021 Mike Winkelmann considered NFTs an "nonsensical extravagance bubble". By mid-April 2021, request died down, making costs fall fundamentally. Monetary scholar William J. Bernstein contrasted the NFT market with seventeenth century tulip insanity, saying any speculative air pocket requires a mechanical development for individuals to "become amped up for", with a piece of that energy coming from the outrageous expectations being made about the item.

Edit with WPS Office

Tax evasion

NFTs, as with other blockchain protections and with conventional workmanship deals, might possibly be utilized for illegal tax avoidance. Closeout stages for NFT deals might confront administrative strain to consent to hostile to illegal tax avoidance regulation. Gou Wenjun, the overseer of the Anti-Money Laundering Monitoring and Analysis Center for the People's Bank of China, communicated that NFTs could "undoubtedly become illegal tax avoidance apparatuses." Gou expounded that there is expanding unlawful abuse of different new cryptographic advancements, and that unlawful entertainers frequently self-distinguish as trailblazers of the monetary innovation area.

A February 2022 review from the United States Treasury surveyed that there was "some proof of tax evasion risk in the high-esteem workmanship market," including through "the arising computerized craftsmanship market, like the utilization of non-fungible tokens (NFTs)." The review thought about how NFT exchanges might be a more straightforward choice for laundering cash through craftsmanship by keeping away from the transportation or protection complexities in exchanging actual workmanship. A few NFT trades were named as virtual resource specialist co-ops that might be dependent upon Financial Crimes Enforcement Network guidelines. In March 2022, two individuals were charged for the execution of a $1,000,000 NFT plot through wire misrepresentation.

Different purposes

Edit with WPS Office

In 2019, Nike protected a framework called CryptoKicks that would utilize NFTs to confirm the realness of actual shoes and would give a virtual variant of the shoe to the client.

Occasion tickets have been proposed available to be purchased as NFTs. This would empower occasion coordinators or entertainers to earn sovereignties on resales.

Norms in blockchains

Explicit symbolic norms support different blockchain use-cases. Ethereum was the first blockchain to help NFTs with its ERC-721 norm and this is currently[may be obsolete as of March 2022] the most broadly utilized. Numerous other blockchains have added or plan to add support for NFTs.

ERC-721 was the main norm for addressing non-fungible advanced resources on the Ethereum blockchain. ERC-721 is an inheritable Solidity shrewd agreement standard; "inheritable" implies that designers can make new ERC-721-consistent agreements by duplicating from a reference execution. ERC-721 gives center techniques that permit following the proprietor of a one of a kind identifier, as well as a permissioned way[clarification needed] for the proprietor to move the resource for other people.

The ERC-1155 standard offers "semi-fungibility", as well as giving

Edit with WPS Office

a simple to ERC-721 usefulness (implying that an ERC-721 resource can be fabricated utilizing ERC-1155). Dissimilar to ERC-721 where a remarkable ID addresses a solitary resource, the exceptional ID of an ERC-1155 token addresses a class of resources, and there is an extra amount field to address how much the class that a specific wallet has. Resources of a similar class are exchangeable, and a client can move any measure of resources for other people.

Edit with WPS Office

CHAPTER FIVE

Why Are NFTs Becoming Popular?

NFTs have really been around starting around 2015, however they are presently encountering a lift in notoriety because of a few elements. In the first place, and maybe most clearly, is the standardization and energy of cryptographic forms of money and the basic blockchain systems. Past the actual innovation is the mix of being a fan, the financial matters of eminences, and the laws of shortage. Purchasers all need to get in on the chance to claim exceptional computerized content and possibly hold them as a kind of speculation.

At the point when somebody purchases a non-fungible token, they gain responsibility for content, however it can in any case advance over the Internet. Along these lines, a NFT can acquire prevalence – the more it's seen on the web, the more worth it creates. At the point when the resource is sold, the first maker gets a 10 percent cut, with the stage getting a little rate and the ongoing proprietor getting the remainder of that income. Consequently, there is potential for progressing income from well known computerized resources as they are traded over the long haul.

Validness is the situation with NFTs. Computerized collectibles contain recognizing data that make them unmistakable from some other NFT and effectively obvious, on account of the

Edit with WPS Office

blockchain. Making and coursing counterfeit collectibles doesn't work in light of the fact that every thing can be followed back to the first maker or guarantor. Also, dissimilar to digital forms of money, they can't be straightforwardly traded with each other (like baseball cards, in actuality) on the grounds that no two are something similar.

All in all, with all the fight made over NFTs, is it precise to say that they're presently standard? This article presents major areas of strength for a for accepting that NFTs are currently prepared into the public cognizance. It doesn't hurt that various high-profile big names have wandered into NFT waters.

While maybe it very well might be untimely to say "OK, NFTs are most certainly standard now," assuming they forge ahead with this direction, 2022 could be the year where we realize that NFTs are staying put.

How is a NFT Different From Other Cryptocurrencies?

Despite the fact that NFTs are made involving similar sort of programming language as other cryptographic forms of money, that is where the comparability closes.

Other Cryptocurrency

Edit with WPS Office

NFT

Digital currencies are "fungible"; they can be exchanged or traded for each other. They're additionally equivalent in esteem.

For instance, one Bitcoin is generally equivalent to another Bitcoin, or one Dollar is dependably equivalent to one Dollar.

Each NFT goes about as a computerized signature that makes it inconceivable for them to be traded for or equivalent to each other.

For instance, The Last Supper is a painting of a sort and can't be traded with another painting.

Ethereum and NFTs

Ethereum blockchain makes it feasible for NFTs to work because of multiple factors:

Exchanging NFTs, without requiring shared stages, can accept critical cuts as pay.

All Ethereum items share something similar "backend", making NFTs compact to purchase on one item and sell it on another easily.

When an exchange is affirmed, it's difficult to control the information to fashion the possession.

Ethereum never goes down, and that implies your tokens will continuously be accessible to sell.

Penguin Communities

Plump Penguin is a famous non-fungible symbolic local area, a digital money subcategory addressing possession in a remarkable resource: 8,888 penguins on the Ethereum blockchain, coordinated into one assortment. Plump Penguin is only one of numerous networks out there that deal benefits and different benefits to individuals, for example, having an enrollment on a common Discord server or accessing a confidential Telegram station that allows you to converse with different proprietors.

Numerous NFT projects have their own networks, where individuals can work together, share thoughts, and backing or get each other's ventures or craftsmanship.

How to Buy NFTs?

Having perceived what NFTs are utilized for and its particular benefits over other digital currencies, you should wander into

Edit with WPS Office

purchasing NFTs. Provided that this is true, you should obtain a few fundamental things before you make it happen:

You'll require a computerized wallet that permits you to store your NFTs and digital currencies.

Then you really want to buy some cryptographic money relying upon what monetary forms your NFT supplier acknowledges, in all likelihood Ether. You can utilize stages like OpenSea, Coinbase, Kraken, PayPal, and so on, to purchase digital forms of money.

Whenever you've made your digital currency buy, you can move it from the trade to your wallet.

Remember, that many trades charge a little level of your crypto buy exchange as expenses.

Famous NFT Marketplaces

Whenever you have your wallet prepared, all you really want to do is to purchase NFT. Right now, the biggest NFT commercial centers are:

Rarible - Rarible is a popularity based commercial center that permits craftsmen and makers to issue and sell NFTs. It empowers holders to say something regarding highlights like charges and local area rules.

Edit with WPS Office

NFT has upgraded media openness and exceptional advantages for hopeful craftsmen via web-based entertainment. As of late, Jack Dorsey, the CEO and fellow benefactor of Twitter, with his absolute first and renowned tweet, "simply setting up my twttr," and Vignesh Sundaresan, broadly known as "Metakovan," purchased 69.3 million bucks worth of NFT workmanship on Beeple.

Attributable to its rising fame, individuals are presently able to pay countless dollars for NFTs.

Like David Gerard, creator of Attack of the 50-foot Blockchain, numerous specialists in the crypto business express that around 40% of new crypto clients will involve NFTs as their entrance point. Because of its developing prominence, NFT could address a more critical piece of the computerized economy later on.

Since the items in NFTs are openly available, anyone can undoubtedly duplicate a document referred to by a NFT. Besides, the responsibility for NFT on the blockchain doesn't intrinsically pass legitimately enforceable licensed innovation privileges on to the document.

It has become notable that a NFT picture can be replicated or saved from an internet browser by utilizing a right snap menu to download the referred to picture. NFT allies vilify this duplication

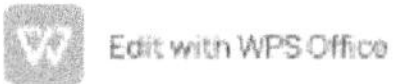
Edit with WPS Office

of NFT craftsmanship as "right-clicker mindset". One gatherer cited by Vice looked at the worth of a bought NFT (rather than an unpurchased duplicate of the fundamental resource) for that of a superficial point of interest "to flaunt that they can bear to pay that much".

The "right-clicker mindset" express spread virally after its presentation, especially among the individuals who were condemning of the NFT commercial center and who appropriated the term to parade their capacity to catch advanced workmanship supported by NFT effortlessly. This analysis was advanced by Australian developer Geoffrey Huntley who made "The NFT Bay", demonstrated after The Pirate Bay. The NFT Bay promoted a deluge record suspected to contain 19 terabytes of computerized workmanship NFT pictures. Huntley contrasted his work with a craftsmanship project from Pauline Pantsdown, and trusted the site would assist with instructing clients on what NFTs endlessly are not.

Capacity off-chain

NFTs that address computerized workmanship for the most part don't store the related fine art record on the blockchain because of the huge size of such a document, and the restricted handling rate of blockchains. Such a symbolic capabilities like a testament of proprietorship, with a web address that focuses to the piece of craftsmanship being referred to; this anyway makes the actual

Edit with WPS Office

workmanship powerless against interface decay.

Ecological worries

See moreover: Environmental effect of digital currencies

NFT buys and deals are empowered by the high energy utilization, and resulting ozone harming substance emanations, related with blockchain exchanges. However all types of Ethereum exchanges affect the climate, the immediate effect of exchange is likewise reliant upon the size of the Ethereum exchange. The evidence of-work convention expected to direct and confirm blockchain exchanges on organizations, for example, Ethereum consumes a lot of power. To gauge the carbon impression of a given NFT exchange requires different suspicions or assessments about how that exchange is set up on the blockchain, the financial way of behaving of blockchain diggers (and the energy requests of their mining hardware), and how much environmentally friendly power being utilized on these organizations. There are additionally calculated questions, for example, whether the carbon impression gauge for a NFT buy ought to consolidate some piece of the continuous energy interest of the fundamental organization, or simply the negligible effect of that specific buy. A relationship may be the carbon impression related with an extra traveler on a given carrier flight.

Some NFT advances use approval conventions, for example, evidence of stake, that utilization significantly less energy per

Edit with WPS Office

approval cycle. Different ways to deal with lessening power incorporate the utilization of off-chain exchanges as a component of stamping a NFT. Various NFT craftsmanship locales desire to address these worries, and some are moving to advancements and conventions with lower related impressions. Others presently permit the choice of purchasing carbon counterbalances while making NFT buys, albeit the natural advantages of this have been addressed. In certain occurrences, NFT specialists have ruled against offering their very own portion work to restrict fossil fuel byproduct commitments. However there are currently "eco-accommodating" NFTs, Ethereum actually overwhelms the NFT market, bringing about an effect on the climate.

Craftsman and purchaser expenses

Deals stages charge specialists and purchasers expenses for stamping, posting, asserting, and optional deals. Examination of NFT markets in March 2021, in the quick result of Beeple's "Everydays: the First 5000 Days" selling for US$69.3 million, found that most NFT craftsmanships were selling for under US$200, with a third selling for under US$100. Those selling NFTs beneath $100 were paying stage expenses somewhere in the range of 72.5% and 157.5% of that sum. On normal the expenses make 100.5% of the cost, implying that such craftsmen were on normal paying more cash in charges than they were making in deals.

Literary theft and extortion

Edit with WPS Office

There have been instances of specialists and makers having their work sold by others as a NFT without authorization. After the craftsman Qing Han passed on in 2020, her character was expected by a fraudster and some of her works opened up for buy as NFTs. Likewise, a vender acting like Banksy prevailed with regards to selling a NFT evidently made by the craftsman for $336,000 in 2021; the merchant discounted the cash after the case drew media consideration. In 2022, it was found that as a feature of their NFT promoting effort, a NFT organization that voice entertainer Troy Baker reported his association with had copied voice lines, a free AI text-to-discourse project created by MIT.

The secrecy related no sweat with which they can be fashioned make it challenging to seek after lawful activity against NFT literary thieves.

Some NFT commercial centers answered instances of literary theft by making "takedown groups" to answer craftsman grievances. The NFT commercial center OpenSea has rejects copyright infringement and deepfakes (non-consensual private symbolism). A few specialists scrutinized OpenSea's endeavors, saying they are delayed to answer takedown solicitations and that craftsmen are likely to help tricks from clients who guarantee to be delegates from the stage. Others contend that there is no market motivator for NFT commercial centers to get serious about literary theft.

Edit with WPS Office

A cycle known as "sleepminting" permits a fraudster to mint a NFT in a craftsman's wallet and move it back to their own record without the craftsman becoming mindful. This permitted a white cap programmer to mint a false NFT that had apparently started from the wallet of the craftsman Beeple.

Copyright infringement concerns drove the craftsmanship site DeviantArt to make a calculation that looks at client workmanship posted on the DeviantArt site against workmanship on well known NFT commercial centers. Assuming the calculation distinguishes craftsmanship that is comparative, it informs and teaches the creator how they can contact NFT commercial centers to demand that they bring down their appropriated work.

The BBC revealed an instance of insider exchanging when a representative of the NFT commercial center OpenSea purchased explicit NFTs before they were sent off, with earlier information those NFTs would be advanced on the organization's landing page. NFT exchanging is an unregulated market where there is no lawful response for such maltreatments.

At the point when Adobe reported they were adding NFT backing to their designs manager Photoshop, the organization proposed making an InterPlanetary File System information base as an elective method for laying out validness for computerized works.

The cost paid for explicit NFTs and the business volume of a specific NFT creator might be falsely expanded by wash exchanging, which is pervasive because of an absence of

Edit with WPS Office

unofficial law on NFTs.

Security

In January 2022, it was accounted for that a NFTs were being taken advantage of by merchants to unconsciously accumulate client IP addresses. The "exploit" works through the off-chain nature of NFT, as the client's PC consequently follows a web address in the NFT to show the substance. The server at the location can then log the IP address and in certain models powerfully adjust the restored content to show the outcome. OpenSea specifically has a more grounded type of this proviso in that it permits HTML records to be connected.

Pyramid/Ponzi plot claims

Pundits look at the design of the NFT market to a pyramid or Ponzi plot, in which early adopters benefit to the detriment of those purchasing in later. In June 2022, Bill Gates expressed his conviction that NFTs are "100 percent in view of more prominent numb-skull hypothesis".

"Floor covering pull" leave tricks

A "floor covering pull" is a trick, like a leave trick or a siphon and dump conspire, in which the designers of a NFT or other blockchain project publicity the worth of an undertaking to siphon up the cost and afterward unexpectedly offer every one of their tokens to secure in enormous benefits or in any case forsake the

Edit with WPS Office

venture while eliminating liquidity, for all time obliterating the worth of the task. Mat pulls have turned into an inexorably normal risk while purchasing NFTs, with the returns of some floor covering pulls being esteemed at many thousands or even huge number of dollars. Mat pulls represented 37% of all crypto-related trick income in 2021, as per one examination.

In summary

On account of this "What is a NFT?" instructional exercise, you have now seen all that you want to be familiar with what a NFT is, the manner by which it works, its purposes, and the way that you can get them.

Edit with WPS Office

CHAPTER SIX

This is a rundown of the greatest realized costs perhaps paid for non-fungible tokens (NFTs) addressing computerized resources.

Adaptation of advanced resources as NFTs became conceivable with the arrival of Etheria, on the Ethereum blockchain, in 2015. Subsequent to building up some decent forward momentum in late 2017, the NFT market filled rapidly in 2020. This went on into 2021, prompting a gigantic purchasing flood, as more than $200 million worth of NFTs were exchanged the initial three months alone.

One of the earliest NFT projects, CryptoPunks, delivered by LarvaLabs on the Ethereum blockchain, has given a few of the most costly NFTs. There were some NFT-like ventures or "proto NFTs" that pre-date CryptoPunks; Rare Pepes, for instance, was delivered on Counterparty in 2014.

Rundown of top craftsmen by deals volume

This rundown depends on the volume of complete potential NFT deals across stages including Nifty Gateway, SuperRare, Foundation, hic et nunc, MakersPlace, KnownOrigin, ArtBlocks and Async Art. Absolute craftsmanship esteem depends on the

Edit with WPS Office

craftsman's market capitalization, not the craftsman's all out deals esteem.

Rank	Artist	Total work of art esteem (USD)	Artworks sold	Highest sale	Average deal
1	Pak	$356,743,178.83	66320	$91,800,000.00	$5,379.20
2	Beeple	$175,588,653.19	1351	$69,346,250.00	$129,969.40
3	Tyler Hobbs	$101,024,939.75	1009	$175,872.55	$100,123.83
4	Dmitri Cherniak	$84,798,496.18	868	$2,682,00.00	$97,694.12
5	XCOPY	$94,679,456.27	9543	$5,344,623.30	$9,921.35
6	mattdesl	$48,771,518.97	2070	$32,856.35	$23,561.12
7	Hackatao	$34,624,985.68	4583	$932,285.00	$7,555.09
8	richlord	$27,465,452.48	1423	$25,356.66	$19,301.09
9	Monica Rizzolli	$26,768,212.51	1026	$26,139.28	$26,089.88
10	FEWOCiOUS	$26,670,333.88	3189	$2,838,640.00	$8,363.23

Edit with WPS Office

Rundown of greatest costs paid

This rundown is requested by shopper cost record expansion changed esteem (in striking) in great many United States dollars in 2021.[note 1] Where vital, the cost is first switched over completely to dollars utilizing the conversion scale at the time the NFT was sold. The expansion change might change, as late expansion rates are frequently reexamined. A rundown in another cash might be in a somewhat unique request because of conversion scale variances. NFTs are recorded just a single time, for example at the greatest expense sold. To keep a reasonable size, just NFTs that were sold at a changed cost of $2 million or more are recorded underneath.

Changed cost

(a large number of US$) Original cost

(a large number of US$) Asset Year of creation Date of sale Seller Buyer Blockchain Notes

$72.6 $69.3 Everydays: the First 5000 Days 2021 March 11, 2021 Beeple Metakovan (Vignesh Sundaresan)[8]Ethereum First piece of simply NFT work of art to be presented by a significant sales management firm Christie's.

$52.7 $52.8 Clock 2022February 9, 2022 Pak AssangeDAO Ethereum Clock is a solitary NFT that portrays a clock, which counts the quantity of days Julian Assange has

Edit with WPS Office

spent in jail and is the most costly NFT sold on-chain.

$30.3 $28.985 HUMAN ONE 2021November 9, 2021 Beeple Ryan Zurrer Ethereum HUMAN ONE is a motor video design with a relating dynamic NFT; and was unloaded at Christie's for $28,958,000.

$23.7 $23.7 CryptoPunk #5822 2017February 12, 2022 Unknown "Deepak" Ethereum Originally Released by Larva Labs. Purchased by Unknown for 1641$. Exchanged almost 5 years after the fact by Unknown for $23,700,000 to "Deepak".

$12.3 $11.75 CryptoPunk #7523 2017June 10, 2021 "Sillytuna" Unknown Ethereum Originally Released by Larva Labs. Sold for $11,754,000 by Sotheby's.

$8 $7.67 CryptoPunk #3100 2017March 11, 2021 Unknown Unknown Ethereum Originally Released by Larva Labs. Sold for 4,200 ETH, day after day 4,200 ETH deal.

$7.9 $7.6 CryptoPunk #7804 2017March 10, 2021 Unknown Unknown Ethereum One of nine Aliens on offer.[failed verification] Originally Released by Larva Labs. Sold for 4200 ETH.

$6.9 $6.60 Beeple's CROSSROAD 2021February 25, 2021 Pablo Rodriguez-Fraile Delphina Leucas (Anonymous pen name) from the first cost of $66666.60 a couple of months sooner in October 2020.

$6.3 $6.034 XCOPY's A Coin for the Ferryman 2018 November 4, 2021 "electricmeat" "jpeggy" Ethereum XCOPY A Coin for the Ferryman is the most noteworthy deal on the Crypto

Edit with WPS Office

workmanship stage, SuperRare, up until this point.

$6.3 $6.0 Beeple's OCEAN FRONT 2021March 22, 2021 Justin Sun Justin Sun Ethereum Auctioned on the Niftygateway stage.

$5.9 $5.59 CryptoPunk #5217 2017July 30, 2021 "Snowfro" Unknown Ethereum Originally Released by Larva Labs in 2017.

$5.7 $5.40 Edward Snowden's Stay Free 2021April 16, 2021 Edward Snowden PleasrDAO Ethereum First NFT by Edward Snowden in the interest of the Freedom of Press Foundation.

$5.5 $5.23 Save Thousands of Lives 2021May 8, 2021 Noora Health Paul Graham Ethereum Sold for 1,337 ETH in this cause sell off.

$4.6 $4.40 Doge (meme) 2021June 12, 2021 Atsuko Sato PleasrDAO Ethereum Highest offering image NFT to date. Sold for 1,696.69 ETH.

$4.6 $4.37 CryptoPunk #2338 2017August 6, 2021 Unknown Unknown Ethereum Published in 2017 by Larva Labs, one of 88 Zombie Cryptopunks.

$4.3 $4.14 Mad Dog Jones' REPLICATOR 2021April 23, 2021 Mad Dog Jones Unknown Ethereum REPLICATOR was the main NFT sell off by Phillips (barkers)

$4 $3.806 XCOPY's Some Asshole 2018September 27, 2021 Unknown Unknown Ethereum Sold for 1,300 ETH on SuperRare.

$4 $3.765 EtherRock #55 2021October 25, 2021 Unknown

Edit with WPS Office

Unknown Ethereum The most noteworthy offer of an Etherrock so far was on October 25, 2021 by means of fractional.art.

$3.6 $3.6 PEPENOPOULOS, 2016 2016October 26, 2021 Unknown Unknown Bitcoin This exceptional Rare Pepe was sold by Sotheby's during the main sale on their "Metaverse", a stage devoted to NFT gatherers,

$3.4 $3.4 BAYC #8817 2021October 26, 2021 Unknown Unknown Ethereum Bored Ape Yacht Club is a NFT workmanship assortment sent off on April 1, 2021, comprising of 10,000 novel works. #8817 is the most costly chimp up until this point.

$3.5 $3.3 Fidenza #313 2021August 23, 2021 Unknown Unknown Ethereum Fidenza stamped on Art Blocks is a Generative Art NFT by Tyler Hobbs.

$3.1 $2.925 XCOPY's All Time High in the City 2018October 12, 2021 Unknown Unknown Ethereum Sold for 1,000 ETH on SuperRare.

$2.9 $2.9 The first Tweet by Twitter CEO Jack Dorsey 2006 March 22, 2021 Jack Dorsey Sina Estavi Ethereum Sold for 1,630.5 ETH. Dorsey gave his returns to the cause GiveDirectly. The tweet was posted on March 21, 2006 at 4:50 PM.

$3 $2.883 EtherRock #27 2017August 28, 2021 Unknown Unknown Ethereum EtherRock is one of the absolute first NFT projects from 2017. 100 Etherrocks exist altogether. Rock #27 was sold for 888 ETH

$2.8 $2.712 EtherRock #73 2017September 7, 2021 Unknown

Edit with WPS Office

Unknown Ethereum EtherRock is one of the absolute first NFT projects from 2017. 100 Etherrocks exist altogether. Rock #73 was sold for 790 ETH

$2.7 $2.6 BAYC #8585 2021 October 19, 2021 Unknown Unknown Ethereum Bored Ape Yacht Club is a NFT craftsmanship assortment sent off on April 1, 2021, comprising of 10,000 remarkable works. #8585 was sold for 696.969.

$2.7 $2.7 Self Portrait #1, 2020 - Dmitri Cherniak 2020 October 26, 2021 Unknown Unknown Ethereum "This generative self representation is the main work in Cherniak's profession." It was sold on Sotheby's "Metaverse" stage.

$2.8 $2.648 Dmitri Cherniak's A slight absence of balance can cause so much pain 2021 October 1, 2021 Dmitri Cherniak Starry Night Capital Ethereum Sale for 800 ETH on SuperRare.

$2.5 $2.413 Beeple's TIME The Future of Business (Beeple Edition) 2021 October 6, 2021 Unknown Starry Night Capital Ethereum The work of art was a cooperation among Beeple and Time magaizine and sold for 675 ETH on SuperRare.

$2.5 $2.382 Refik Anadol's Machine Hallucinations - Space : Metaverse 2021 October 4, 2021 Unknown Unknown Ethereum Sold for 18,325,000 HKD at Sotheby's.

$2.4 $2.268 EtherRock #96 2017 September 2, 2021 Unknown Unknown Ethereum Another offer of an Etherrock this time for 599 ETH ($1,929,060)

$2.1 $2.043 Dreaming at Dusk 2021 March 14, 2021

Edit with WPS Office

Torproject PleasrDAO Ethereum Sold for 500 ETH on Foundation.

$2.1 $2.035 MetaRift 2021 March 15, 2021 Pak Dannysecure Ethereum Sold for 489 ETH on MakersPlace.

$2.1 $2.0 SMB #1355 2021 October 1, 2021 Unknown Unknown Solana This is at present the most noteworthy deal recorded on the Solana blockchain. SMB #1355 has been sold for 13,027.

Edit with WPS Office

CHAPTER SEVEN

We as a whole skill significant digital forms of money are, yet it turns into significantly seriously intriguing on the off chance that you can procure free crypto.

Purchasing crypto with your government issued types of money is an easy decision. There are numerous great digital currency trades and stages for that.

Some likewise take a more specialized course in mining crypto.

Both these techniques are to some degree unsafe, as crypto costs can influence like anything with simply an Elon Musk tweet.

crypto exchanging

Notwithstanding, we are here to educate you concerning a dependable method for stashing some of them without spending anything.

So with no stand by, I'll begin with the rundown portraying stages to procure free crypto.

Edit with WPS Office

Coinbase

There are numerous cryptographic forms of money. At Coinbase, you can find out about a portion of these crypto projects while procuring a couple of tokens.

coinbase-procure free crypto

It's pretty much as straightforward as it sounds, procure while you learn.

The main drawback is that you may not satisfy a portion of the qualification terms except if you move to an alternate country. Along these lines, this program is for chosen nations, and Coinbase is attempting to add more as we talk about it.

Freecash

Freecash accomplices with notices and think-tanks which boost playing out specific assignments.

You can finish these area explicit offers and overviews to get free digital currencies. Then again, one can likewise use Freecash acquired coins as gift vouchers, Counter-Strike Global Offensive skins, and so forth. A few different elements are:

Edit with WPS Office

Moment Crypto cashouts beginning at 0.10$

DOGE, Bitcoin, Litecoin and more

Mess around and complete different errands

Clients acquire more than $20.00 each day on normal on Freecash

For example, this was an overview with the prize sum referenced at the upper right corner:

freecash study

Join is incredibly straightforward; utilize your Google or Steam account. Additionally, you can enroll by email to begin.

Each 1000 Freecash coins equivalent 1 USD.

While standard withdrawals require 5-10 minutes, a PayPal payout can ordinarily require 24 hours to understand. You can utilize Freecash on your work area or cell phone.

They have a valuable FAQ segment that I'll suggest perusing prior to joining.

Coinrabbit

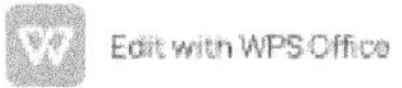
Edit with WPS Office

Coinrabbit is for the individuals who need to get an incredible arrangement with free crypto.

In the event that you as of now have some digital currency, don't have any desire to hold it with no benefit until the rates will increase, and need to make it work for you now, a crypto loaning device is precisely exact thing you really want.

In this manner, the Coinrabbit stage offers you a chance to acquire the most extreme from what you have now to get free crypto and gain free automated revenue.

Fundamentally, you can involve your digital forms of money as guarantee to get a crypto credit, which you can put resources into any resources and uninhibitedly procure from their development. Along these lines, you will save your coins and get additional cash out of the blue.

Utilize your digital currency as guarantee (you can take it back any time you need)

Get free stablecoins

Put your stablecoins into productive resources

Get back your guarantee at the ideal second

Edit with WPS Office

Save for yourself all the additional increase of your guarantee cost increment

Brilliant? - Profitable 💰

Furthermore, for the individuals who need no additional developments, this stage has a smooth method for getting free coins.

You can open an investment account to procure revenue on your cryptographic money. Uninvolved income will top up your equilibrium consistently until you close your bank account. Simultaneously, the assets and your prize will be accessible for withdrawal whenever.

That is all there is to it. Simple.

CoinMarketCap

CoinMarketCap has a comparative learn and procure program for crypto devotees.

coinmarketcap

Yet, it stretches out one stage beyond Coinbase in that it has tests to confirm your insight. What's more, it's not just about

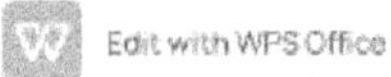
Edit with WPS Office

capability; you need to score an ideal 100 percent to procure crypto free of charge. Moreover, there might be explicit undertakings related with your course.

Furthermore, sadly, CoinMarketCap likewise confines investment from a couple of recorded nations.

Remember, this program capabilities on a the early bird gets the worm premise. In this way, the competitors will just get the tokens until the pre-concluded conveyance sum evaporates.

Coin Hunt World

This is no other course! Coin Hunt World is a Pokemon-go kind of game accessible on Android and iOS. In light of your geo-area, you will stroll around gathering keys, opening boxes, making companions, and substantially more.

Coin Hunt Word assists you with procuring modest quantities of Bitcoin and Ethereum free of charge.

YouTube video

Coin Hunt Worlds is from individuals behind an eminent digital money trade, Bittrex. Furthermore, you can find individuals on

Edit with WPS Office

Reddit looking at procuring 50 to 100 USD each week from it.

All in all, what's the trick?

There is none on the off chance that you're based out of the USA, Canada, the UK, and EL Salvador. Outstandingly, the Philippines is recorded as not far off. Others should stand by till their nation is added.

Crypto PopCoin

Crypto Popcoin is one more game to procure free crypto: Ethereum and PopCoin. The ongoing interaction is straightforward. You need to bunch coins and afterward tap to pop them.

Edit with WPS Office

www.ingramcontent.com/pod-product-compliance
Lightning Source LLC
LaVergne TN
LVHW052103160826
845678LV00015B/3326

* 9 7 9 8 8 4 8 8 1 6 0 0 6 *